Luke Beesley | Jam Sticky Vision

New Poems

GIRAMONDO POETS

Luke Beesley | Jam Sticky Vision

First published 2015
from the Writing & Society Research Centre
at the University of Western Sydney
by the Giramondo Publishing Company
PO Box 752 Artarmon NSW 1570 Australia
www.giramondopublishing.com

Designed by Harry Williamson
Typeset by Andrew Davies
in 10/16.5 pt Baskerville

Printed and bound by Ligare
Distributed in Australia by NewSouth Books

National Library of Australia
Cataloguing-in-Publication data:

Beesley, Luke
Jam Sticky Vision / Luke Beesley
ISBN 9781922146847 (pbk)

A821.3

In a time of confusion and rapid change like the present, when terms are continually turning inside out and the names of things hardly keep their meaning from day to day, it's not possible to write two honest paragraphs without stopping to take crossbearings on every one of the abstractions that were so well ranged in ornate marble niches in the minds of our fathers.

JOHN DOS PASSOS (1935)

Other books by Luke Beesley

Lemon Shark
Balance
New Works on Paper

Acknowledgements

Poems in *Jam Sticky Vision* have been published in *Australian Book Review*, *Arc* (Canada), *Cordite*, *Island Magazine* and *Rabbit* – thank you to the editors. Particular thanks to the supreme *Cordite*, edited by Kent MacCarter. Grateful acknowledgment to the Australia Council for a new work grant to complete this book; and to The Wheeler Centre and The Readings Foundation for a Hot Desk Fellowship where many of these poems were edited, and where 'How Will I Know When I'm Home?' was drafted. 'Open Plan Bird's Nest Roomy Esplanade Theatre' was written for *Cashew the Light*, a collaboration with ceramicist Kate Hill, exhibited at Mr Kitly Gallery, Melbourne, 17 May–2 June 2013; thanks Kate. 'Peacock Peacock' and 'Two Shorts' appeared in the chapbook *Balance* (2012), published by Whitmore Press. Thank you to Nicholas Powell for a careful-close reading and generous feedback, and also to Zoë Miller for readings, design savvy, and all! As ever, gratitude to Ivor Indyk and Alice Grundy for ongoing, nuanced support and editorial guidance.

Contents

A Thousand Characters

after Koch/Cohen, Malley/Breton, Roussel!

This, too, is about a thousand characters. It's much like the last one. I wouldn't even read beyond the following sentence. The following sentence is a silky thing – purple in the late day, drizzled in smog. Inside a microwave oven is milk rising to warmth. Inside the dusk is an excuse for certain birds to frolic on the freshly-cut lawn too long, picking at insects. They're eaten by sparrow-hawks. It's pretty gruesome. The rugby team on their regular jog start slipping on the mess of birds. From a distance it looks like a scrum or naval exercise. It's getting dark remarkably quickly and the clouds, just above the line of trees which form the horizon, here, are salmon-pink. At the local gelati shop they'd call it grapefruit. Navy tinges fringe the pale pink. Fish await. It's beyond human understanding how someone might have reached this sentence. I could write about pork. The sparrow hawk eats well and feeds the parts of its name to its young, and its young feed parts of their own name to their first flight. Nature as documentary, now, and it's where we slip. See the magpie on the end of my sandwich? It knew it was to be written, probably, and it curved here like a ball in a stadium. But there is no crowd, bird, alone in the credits. Some gaffers. Giraffes with appalling foot rot trot over to the microphone and discoball concussions the wild shining toffee of the dance floor on this afternoon as the moon pierces in.

Retreating Moods

the fatigue attuned to used
car dealers' unbuckled vermillion

racing postures or driver's side opinions un
folding maps larger than the interior
of the rally car

as in Morris Louis
his paintings were larger than the room
he made them in

Your Margin, My Mahjong

A short way and a beautiful pale bone-rough fencing or pipeline. The soft, too, cigarette smoke of Rothko's moustache ends up in hospital – two journeys admitted into one rectangle. Like this one, here – I hope for it to become a square. I admit to melancholy encounter, touched up photograph – tweezer/pixel the only known genotype/trope or genome/existence. *Existenz* (1999). I refuse to sit and listen to exquisite sounds provided by night insects and traffic on the highway four kms away. Arbour.

The Australian Double

This opening in an American accent and living abroad for the length of this note, years. It's gradually receding, the r's softening, disappearing, even. Say birds (floating in on this reminiscence).

The imitation leaves of Edinburgh Gardens in the back of my mind with my aunt's death and my cousins' stoic resistance. Any mention of cancer and the couch is lost under numerous throws. Can't remember the colour of it. Grey, an indiscriminate beige. The back of my mind with the first memories of this country – the air alive at night with insects.

Pawpaw just ahead of cool afternoon breezes, Brisbane afternoon.

Dog chains pulled the dining table until the parched afternoon vanished in a dusk pack.

The dogs piled on top of the wood that father had killed and made tennis shoes.

The table he rented from the bank which hounded him weekly impersonating friends to get him to open mail practises signature.

I took his signature to mean originality in the first light of his undreamt future.

She Came In Through or The Bathroom Window

after Paris, Texas

Her dress plagiarised
the footpath, gravelly thin.
Pretty quatrains it came in.

His signature tied her to
the oven and went drinking,
calmly.

In mouths we place our hands
in hoops we disappear.

Broken Onset Circles

One thing follows another awning on the event horizon. The horizon itself a distant fact is an awning itself is an open window here, she says, and I reach it. The carpet grass pulls from under me like a wrung-out bed sheet. Lions asleep. A lion on the horizon snap sugarcane smothers the tourist's lip and the warm vat of sun on his cheek warps his chin.

Op Shop

If, for the purpose of a noun in a door

way, hunched, I'm reading and the field
reads and the rain, over there, begins

a new page. This is a page out of George Oppen

's carpark. He's eliminating dust – sticky
corners no one could open the aluminium door!

Sun Blistered

made clear shadows. I cut my feet
on. It cut across the driveway

all over fences they were
my shoulders and the bough

of my arm up towards the painful rip
e light.

The Apology

And then one of the more fascinating especially stories to have theatrical numerous periodicals, the pages of the thinnest individual pages of one or two discarded café newspapers, were stuck to a treetrunk directly opposite the numerous theatrical cafe atmospheres having been one-at-a-time and from front-to-editorial, picked up by the North Sea breeze. Page 1, suddenly, burst like gull, shrewd, chip-in-the-mouth cigarette burned lazy and the two of us follow the pure white dove-like gull departing, like smoke, to describe their nicotine feeling in running writing. That is to peel/appeal those wisps of description further from silly breathing. And it resembles that individual news section. What did you get, breather? Your breathers are a collective, discerning bunch. And this caught on that same breeze as she knelt, hands in the earth, and it came to me illuminated by the word, surprising, rudely, and I went inside. Slabs of desiccated atmosphere, at the time, the one-at-a-time atmosphere, involved in slabs of afternoon thrown against the walls of the kitchen repaired the flowerbed after that beautiful storm, were something of a signature to end, end-to-end. I'd like to take that mood of dove-like, or the music of running writing – just audible breeze or itch, meeting point of front garden and the finger of a branch, and the linen, thinking – and offer you something – a curl of bark, chocolate, my seated help, edits, the communion of weeding

– as an apology.

Drive

In what corners of the poem are hands? Repeated illicit
consonants, statistically. Is it an expression of moodlift or

takeoff fortified with Russian silver cornerstones we
arrive at and decide to keep inside a jamsticky vision?

A Half Hour into Our Conversation

I notice a spoon in her hair. Lucky a copy arrived and
my half of the sugar in my mind, suddenly. PowerPoint-
garish slickerblue and indiscriminately I could feel the
warmth of her head on the spoon clearing her airspace
spices of irritation ground in ceramic/built bowls deeper in
her nonconscious thought (which is an accepted, she says,
recommended expression of the place below consciousness –
no longer *un* but *non*). My hands disembark, and the broken
conversation attempts to sally its way back to our rhythm,
not lost, open to aside, tomorrow, and shifting on and away.

Nude Descending a Solo

Cut page dessert knife salsa at the hour of lunch like pepper pressed tightly in a casual walk, buckled, under the questions. The waitress accommodated against potato, his acumen and silky argument 'admired', he claimed, his knife and for fucking the day harlequin geometrics at the trailing tie. I tried to adjective a closure. Pure 10 minutes inside statistics and they bent like italics. Or should we say during? A band of fat against steak or oily hands. The waitress' eye shadow wrens trained to tie her shoelaces running errands her school was abused and diluted through the streets confettied with the smell of coriander and muffler fume.

The Particular Pace of Writing

Greeted as an apostle of the game, the player purses his lips – smells the egg in his moustache mid-afternoon and exclamation marks pierce the storm clouds. Spectators watch his excess from the other side of frosted windows – rosy harlequin flourishes hovering round the lipstick mark of the football. I turn away and search the room for a precise flower arrangement. My throat thickens. Bangladesh quivers under the real anticipated flooding in the coming century, sneezing! I hope to return to the game but it has trivialised to the point of real importance. My son faints and obliterates his left ear on the corner of a coffee table.

A Piece For the Purpose, Only, of Accentuating 'Pinker'

She was invited to sit for him, and he put
his hand in a brown paper bag. He motion

ed to her to rise, and she came a step closer. He had
a handful of small brushes and began painting her

arms. She collapsed. The bandage he used to align her

elbow was a later brushstroke the colour of a paper bag,
pinker. She had a coffee. They didn't speak, other than to
get on a

bus and visit friends, arriving late with garden flowers and a
trampoline, in the backyard, nieces leaping into a cloud, the
photograph. In the morning she, shaped like an L, shivered,
and they paused and continued again when her husband
arrived, sheepishly, at the window, putting his hand into his
woollen slipper and removing a dead mouse. He'd walked in
the slippers most of the morning thinking the mouse was a
kid's sock. She bargained and the husband watched, and her
hands were painted. She was a nurse.

Carriages

I lift/huge arms of a cobweb/out of the air/and carry its Y/slowly to the porch

MICHAEL ONDAATJE

I was swimming and the air seemed thin and I panicked, there, suddenly, because I realised the shallower dream, the original – a painting on the wall glimpsed – was set in the future.

I was very much alive then and the vines that hung in the surface dream tangled in among the second, the sea, and caused something of a current. What was absent was the double r in either, and the lack of structure in the deeper sea for the vine to attach to. It made for nomenclature, language, a plea for it – defence.

I can only get up walk to the nearest town and order loaves of bread and use them as a pillow to further fall, again, to sleep, in a thicket.

Ironing for half an hour. Absent in the task I burn my finger on the fringe of dreaming, and fog rises off the ocean. I'm impossibly still, without a yacht, and yet the word is lodged in my throat like taking the alphabet, carefully, from a generous spiderweb and carrying it back inside to the kitchen table where all civilization seemed to display itself – that blue table's worn edges. Cracks, peeling paint. I sat there.

The table was there, opening my eyes. Curls of chocolate, coffee in the breakfast bowl. My hands grasp it, the bed of a potted plant. If I draw a picture, dreaming, would it resemble the botanical characteristics of flowers? Or is it harbours, pens, or hangers reserved for enormous warplanes? This, the menace beneath the loaves, deeply sleeping in the midst of a grocer's checkpoint (they have a son ((these retailers)) and the son follows in their profession, unquestioning like a dream within the dream, the grandfather's complexion rising and falling in him through his life, lived in this shop, by the relentless fact of the sea).

The Master

after the 2012 film

Cabbages & the sea
Cabbages & the sea
Cabbages & the sea in PT

The colour of cabbages & the sea
in PT
& the colour of cabbages
& the sea
& the colour
& the cabbages
& the colour
& the sea
& the cabbages of colour
& the sea
& the cabbages of colour
& the sea
& the cabbages
& PT

Cabbages & the sea
Cabbages & the sea
Cabbages & the sea

Cabbages & the sea
Cabbages & the sea

Cabbages & the sea in PT
The colour of cabbages & the sea
The colour of cabbages & the sea
The colour of cabbages & the sea
in PT

Colour of the sea & then the colour of cabbages
Colour of the sea & then the colour of cabbages
Colour of the sea & then the colour of cabbages
& PT

The blue green sea & the blue green cabbage
The blue green sea & sixteen minutes later
The colour of the blue green cabbage

& the blue green sea & then sixteen minutes later
The colour of the blue green cabbage
in PT

After that wild scene strangling
The cabbage of the round married man's portrait
After the twisted scene drinking fuel &

Twisting nipples on the beach in the army
After sea bitten sexing
Garments sales lady in the dark-

Room falling sea asleep later clearly at dinner

At the cabbage Near the habit
At the cabbage Near the habit
At the cabbage Near the habit

At the sea That sandcastle lady &
At the sea That sandcastle lady &
At the sea That sandcastle lady &

The colour of aftershave & the majority of blue skies on cloudless
Cabbage coloured days & the sea infused beaches &
Cabbage coloured uniforms & the sea
Announcements & cocktails

Colour of the sea in cabbage
Colour of the sea in cabbage
Colour of the sea in cabbage

In the cab
In the cab
In the cab

Paul Thomas Anderson &
Philip Seymour Hoffman &
Paul Thomas Anderson &
Philip Seymour Hoffman &
Paul Thomas Anderson &

Philip Seymour Hoffman &
Paul Thomas Anderson &
Philip Seymour Hoffman

New Zealand
New Zealand
New Zealand
New Zealand
New Zealand
New Zealand
New Zealand
New Zealand

Peacock Peacock

Connaught Place, Delhi

In Tagore's last poems he imagines words popped of meaning
loose, in the sky, nonsense syllables, pure colour

At the post office I watch a man for an hour
sew my parcels with a large needle
a purple full stop on his thumb

I never saw the Taj Mahal

I write I never saw the Taj Mahal
but write 'sew' instead of 'saw'
I never sew

Days in the Wake

after Kelly Reichardt

And every morning I write for 15 minutes in a cafe on the edge of the inarticulate museum. Lake. The water sings to the homeless and laps and burns under the one great cloud of Egyptian cotton which we usher forward over the jagged fringe of pine and aspidistra. Sometimes, keenly, 10 min. Or if pressed I could write to the traffic and lift to overpass thinking freely of, and inside, the ushered cloud/insubstantial Japanese ritual. High squeak of sunlight caught on the radio wave. Pitched and nasally as Nick Drake duck-smudged and the surface of the lake turned from a taught cobalt insulation or tarpaulin. My family diagnose the surface of the lake as the dogs and the duck snap and inconsistencies disappear into the next few days of emptied-out joy.

On Balance

India isn't pure anecdote it crumbles in my telling like a poor
motor. Three men came to my door daily to clean my studio
    – swatting,

sweeping and towelling cricket talk. I never knew where
    to stand
hat I said reflected in what swept up leaves and charcoal
    powders

I came to sit near and nudge against open notebooks made
    at markets
the end of a stray bus we run alongside and leap onto.
    I broke my leg

in my anecdote, a shrewd donkey etc. Portuguese tarts that
    articulate
articulate texture of a wet scab.

Six Minute Mark

The mangled sneeze she produced appeared decadent opera beard dog eared page 36 pants through to a third sitting, deficient, distracting actor walked over to the salt basin. Walked for six days handsome got ugly on seven rescued lived out his days as a wind-bitten tax broker. Some maths saved rheumy-eyed scenes of salt-basin record covers. He was left to wait out the pickup which was a day late and foul breath he found deep in his left sleeve revealed the extent of his watery intestine. His orange fall. A blue Fairlane. An overall draped across the ambulance's bonnet. Wacky nurse stoicism avuncular nail polish decoration codes and pickled insects imported in a lunchbox nursing chopsticks and a newspaper report on his own record pursuit.

Scene

Shone in the Middle of Norway

the hourglass on the hour
and the owl stepped like a show horse
into the kitchen

in Picasso and also Oslo
and *The Late Great Townes Van Zandt* played
on the radio

An Ear Out of the Wheat and Right Into T/his Moment

over-inflated jumping castles
wheeze into clowns'
fanta-coloured hair

jostling the whole auditorium
asleep – crisp air
conditioning crackling

First Fourteen Minutes

Tree of Life, Terrence Malick

A muffled goat the powder
eyelash of a cow, half a foot off the ground the film begins
icingblue onelength dress

Eames light rectangles
flooding the open patio caretaker light cool lawn open
fireplace, here, on her

cheeks ruffled by the military
coffeemaker airforce polish jewellery sunlight jewellery death
in the jewellery, narration

pain will pass in time, critique
and pages turning tuning the

sparrows mimic Morris Louis' piano or the phrases Woolf
name Jessica Chastain. spoke through in the waves

Double Portrait, Cornflake Sunset

after Bill Callahan

Characters on set, hours since make-up. It is hard to create through new pain. Old pain buffers it, props it up mahogany tabletop red as a gelding in a slow trot up to the house. Gets off, walks up to the porch. Stops. Takes off his shoes. Walks through the open doorway and the floorboards down the hallway shine like a river in the late afternoon. He eats custard. He has cream pants on and wipes his hands turns his watch over in his head until he stops, walks away from the stove, the tail of his shirt spilling with flame if you put flame into a poem it will help. Help.

Split in the Table

There was a split in the middle of the table. I can't tell you how they avoided it with a lampshade taken from a netball skirt illuminated Georgia and those Russian émigrés displaced on the dessert spoon balancing on their nose in a water feature. The split in the table was so prominent it marinated the walking trails of conversation to keep fit and, attempt to, righteously, remain, one could say, anonymous from the crack itself. They were all but running their fingers over it like the now clichéd illustrations of native flora and fauna on a coin or local dollar note. His lip lifted as if attached by a fishing hook. Her lips pursed, energetically, and the smell of woodsmoke woodsmoke spoke to them like a father train out on the walking tracks or the further line it followed towards clipped dog-eared tiles of paper and sea salt. It gave the meeting an informality, the mix of fragrance, that wasn't rude but his hand was out towards her moving painstakingly backwards and forwards which was misinterpreted back and forth, or even scandalised across. Here, the table hadn't existed, affected. It was really shading like ambiguous unwashed spaniels taken for walks near Skinflint Park and textured air from the nearby sawmills floated in, itself, dogs nudging and jerking their owners through bottlebrush and sycamore, eucalyptus, all there – the while – as a table idea. A cloud. Machetied by a sharp mountain peak. New topography either side of ranges, the great divide, sexes. One – straight-backed, fastidious, sensitive; the other – nervously, self-consciously, slouching. A sloth in tight jeans and uncombed hair, manicured pubis, neat beard, brill cream, lipstick, all brooch and circles – ear, table, idea. It appears they had been walking for some time.

Type Slowly

Concrete walls were a backdrop to the panic
anorak she wore, Tuesday. In the present

skirt she stayed whole minutes – pancakes
– around the table there was a bell pepper

she trusted, looked at the reef, went to Thailand
Her shift was vacant and the other waitresses

meandered in attitudes reflected in the beer-
coloured bottles, their own crisp gypsy
accoutrements. I have such a flimsy

understanding of most adjectives she said
such a flimsy this and left
and I said good

waves create the shore
I must have
muttered or headed neatly fewer and fewer

examples of courtesy and its spilled promises,
wan hunger. Guessing in this film I will follow her
tan put my hands into her dusk-burnt silhouette.

Apricot

The air is ripe as apricots peaking at the end of summer

the sun is apricot over broken chairs. His apricot swear
violence his apricot teeth during and within the

clean up mute as the pure seed surprisingly soft with his
children asleep in his own idea like the seed is, again,

I don't mean to repeat – or put up with – it.

Black and Brown Blues

after David Berman

Impressionistic conversation about the weather – fancy cold swells rolling in on intimacies and the first light of the second and third time they, meta-talking, took (spittle-bubbling on 'the' and 'circumstance') it slowly, afternoon, listening to Royal Trux on rotation at the rink. Neither of them could skate but at some point they moved out across the streaked complexion and entered a fistfight over her skirt, his silly shoes, rusty scent of blood arcing from his teeth, a moment in Francis Bacon, mauve-pink era, late, in his era, in the day, noon, nursing his wonderful mouth mouth. She bent or knelt into him, N, and they finally opened their clothes to third impressions, Manet exhibit, a flagrant documentary, exploited fitness over it or exploitative burnt frosted penguin green decorations of or to or for the credits, period.

After Norwegian Wood

a film by Tran Ahn Hung

he finally arrived at
the asylum he had sex with
he waited

this was his first flassss-

sssssh! back uniform
eating peeled
tangerines apples

her hair was exclamation
smokeinthetrees

(oral)

she cooks two boiled eggs
he pulls on a scab

snow stuck
to her moving like
fruit flies

he slept
in the mouth of a sea-whipped rock
descending tuba, strings (grand prix)

(at this point laughter broke out in the cinema)

he spoke to her using his lunch
she replied with a tight haircut

he sat reading next to her went home
her appointment was an apartment
they sat near the walls

he wiped his bowl she used
her pet

it grew tame
swimming light hit his falcon
t-shirt
a purple necktie floated her cocktail
she

lay
naked back to his guilty
slow, long fish in the margin

his leather belt followed her Coca-Cola
hair
after masturbating

him in strong wind

swimming trunks capsicum they
simultaneously lift

back

out

of

the

pool

in

slo

mo

Wan Erotic

The stubbornness in him recalled the full stop. Under the microscope it resembled another book. And, if that, what of the whole night? By the end of the sentence it was night – full stop. So I went to sleep. For example, and woke in a capital. I could have said mood but are you? Eye or bee. This poem obstructs Egypt in the memory of spelling. I decided to go for a walk and at the end it was, again, night, or really dark and I had a light. I convinced a chiropractor to go deeper – scale down to the floor of the ocean. Again, full stop. The patio of thought was the pallor of her wetness/ patina or intaglio print, at her hips, and throughout the letter we turned and that specific sound the mouth makes around double you, or is it yew? Not enough to blow a candle out, but a thought at least. Palomino.

Ears Scrunched/Up Paper

We were walking towards the vet

I fell on the pillow of the dog
it was Wednesday, its sound

It was so late
I knew we needed the vet
we neared that corner, there were no lights

Someone was pushing a broom
and they looked up,

we were the police,
and came over to the form of the dog

Can I help you? My police dog is hurt. What happened?
I fell on it. Over there and pointed and we glanced up
the road

The House, Eighth Year

Otways

I parked unusually – tucked close to the house out of the branchfall reach of the pines. The thin neat snow-like rain dusted the lawn mistily.

After letting myself in and unpacking the car the force of familiarity in the house began to take me. For a short time. Or was it coming out of the mangled world to the shapes of this routine? The path, the smell of old dust.

I walked inside and for the first seconds running my eyes over the untuned piano, the rim of the doorway to the rooms, the queen above the fireplace, I could see these things last, without the diligence of memory's self protection – compartmentalisation. Porsche. Words I had not been able to decipher here decipher, went back over, protection, compartmentalisation, adding decorative tails to a busted e, or loops to their eyelids.

Receipts had lain in a pocket through the wash, and were mangled against each other in a letter to a good friend. How good? I couldn't make out the name. I'm hardly able to pronounce street names since my hair was flour. It had even come down to my cheek bones, snow on my shoes we siphoned into a breeze dispatch which we cooked for the afternoon in a matinee I saw on the edge of my computer while breaking toast in a ritual of arrival. They mimicked the moustache, easily, which was also a bit itchy.

I found myself in the yard. A year later. The sun lay on my arms like a guilt. A wallaby had been nibbling on my beard. All I could see was the tincture of its paper sides and its pumping cotton legs as I woke up in the bushes and fell in my own jeans. These are the Roman inconsistencies surrounding the open door, spotless house, which were discussed at the annual meeting. Guilty sunlight brassy on the trumpet of the fence paling, gate latch gate latch across the driveway on the highway.

Festival Chat with Peter Craven

A cyclone entered his hair. Trim lines,
office blocks, and season hazard tragic even

ings crisp summer beer moving elegantly in
Gerald Murnane's beer in numerous novels of his.

Sitcoms

i.

often ordinary in folded clothes, a paper plane
occurrence out of her robe and twin beside tables

bedside tables. divorce. an argument out of wife, like thrushes
rushes, further or father and his television which

is larger than his oven, fireplace or three-seater couch
electrical storms.

ii.

is forbidden to dress expectantly, or to
undress on a highway. he pulls over

takes off his jumper after tangling himself
in the glovebox he finds a lamb, followed by a CD

bill callahan. he slowly screws a nut into each tyre
tyres letting them down, gently. an asterisk

of sunlight tensing
on the upholstery.

After Lynch

The hawks beat the other birds and Charlie Parker played chainsaw the night jittery in the documentary the film rolled like a riverfish swam up through dinner under titanium cutlery and tiny coriander art suffice the roundball game perfectly soldiered ear canal where the apple chequered boys dropped kicks with their fathers. I accept I accept the song skipped. Ballooning spinnaker face saxophone discomfort. But I couldn't read in the canoe or spell parchment rhyme in a local theatre spittle restaurant Assange a melody waits to take its part in the poem with garnish inconsistent jazz or weeds press conferences. Press. Hot condom purple sticker more mountain bubble news cable. Get your big leg off me, Buddy Bolden. Warm chocolate beverage and the gulfstream replete on reflection sundressed sentimental afterthought nostalgia bus pickup rice crop. I know a woman. Listened hard. Expert reflection listening buckle back soft passé acknowledgement, mirroring, and I thought political!

You Wanted Me to Return to Writing le Poème About

after Being John Malkovich

there's
something in your eye so I
touch it on the balcon

y you're hosing felled banana
cake off Maxine's lap

I can't write with
out make it up

I'm in the mirror
and have removed

watch the second drawer
it's old

trick I tie crocodile band
s into your hair

as you lecture them o
n no you want me to

write first and
pronoun was supposed to
wait at the lights

Watching Sundance

Ooh that lovely persimmon glint to the snow in bright sunshine – winter.

Jogging along it. He was jogging along it with a headband on, blood dripping from his ears – no...tomato-red headphones.

Blood thrusts through his body, tho, and he stops running and phones his mother. His mother on the other end of the line. Where are our confident men? Offering confident toasts. Entering the room the buttery sun. Burnt edges of a conversation, grey hooded sweater.

Where is Catherine Keener? We need that acid, that humour in our toasts.

Playing pool so far into that green we become our own cocktail.

Her eyebrows snapped, like crust. Who said that?

Jogging alongside her stripes. She darts into a snowstorm, injured wildlife – a soundtrack. Fog horn. Listen to the architecture, the bridge expanding with the touch of midday sun. Skyblue collar peeping out of brown vest. I guess you'll walk into a glacier with a broken fibula?

The music we arranged with a horse's tail. My violin's worse. When the glacier melts it melts into that horse's overcoat, which again swims the snow, which begets the river, which waits for rain.

Where is your range, Catherine?

Calf in the Woods

His capitalised handwriting was artistic, his signature rare among estate agents its electricity and sureness. He would sell a home to my uncle who moved in next door with his farmer's hands and brother's car. It was a sedan. We dreamed to stretch our memory between two thoughts and her insomnia came from the fear of the inevitable loss of her own thoughts as the tumour grew.

Two Shorts

Pinhole

The shimmering sphere on the floor as the sun is interrupt
ed by the round brown cushion on the wicker sitter

Exit

green light I found a word in

Open Plan Bird's Nest Roomy Esplanade Theatre – with ceramicist, Kate Hill

and the wind taking blue scoops out of the air
JOHN BANVILLE, 'Ancient Light'

the circle
came through cashewed

the wheel continued
picking it up apricot

the wet clay at my
Drops
turn/edit
removes the foot,
circle with a fine-point needle to centre
a gust of wind
Oh, O
gentle halting
'sing', turn

Chunky Mauve

the hound moved under
the window like a river broken
loose pane, psychological,
to the dancer, opening their

shoulders held with the tips
of fingers the cool air
inside the house let out
now through the squeaking rusty

window.

Jeans on Last Night's Cheesecake

A line on the survey freeway passover overpass past the milk bar and poultry marine fish decorated fish logical bicycles schooling the corner of the patch. I am not bothered by these seconds and I rally these little seconds with the end of season/ season two. Knots and tendons suffocated by commerce, swollen hedges numerous trees sprouting from my ears where I sit, and, for it, play rough guitar in a 70s pool scene replicated readily in recent Sundance. Or we are a vehicle. My daydream said I was asleep until the topography sans serif entered focus on the laundromat window. Wish. Give it. Honey in our breakfast, grease/increase it. Slowly, fizz and sadly. Think it. Outside on topic ontology!

Words such as Ordinary or Ordinate (Constraint)

after Finnegans Wake

Prop boundary portal node
enfant incorrigible cohort
slather porous nascent inordinate

slouch for uncoordinated
haberdashery treacle irrelevance.
Pulchritudinous lovers mock

fuck on soldier whirr &
sales role boules prop-
ortionate wrestle only

rusted unsentimental illusory
vested participant shore direction
float pack pebble socket

arm pitch reference muscle.
Half stich encyclopaedic
oration stand up

or pitch dark half after-
noon correlation psych
stitch up? Blue wick scar

hours tone dig three
section carpark
anecdote which, over

secretariat blunder, for
shibboleth coronary flake
shop newspaper

inarticulate, comes for
ache-ended titter
section aggregate sum up.

Parlour armour, ours
tourers, fox lick irregular nail
polish ordinate ocular stop.

Unwelcome Lycra /
Portrait of a Patron with a Straw, Loafer

cnr St Georges Rd & Scotchmer

i.

Half a metre from a calf,
cycle – frightened & tanned,

flexing opine occupy politics
with a cracked bat – he seems to

know everyone in the bakery. His
argument (buttered, smoothed &

neatly we shake hands he) invites
me to the park for a game. I put

my hand into my loaf & refuse –
tuck it under my arm. Running

shoes & sourdough, a simulacrum.
I want, here, to reply. I want argument,

fey. But have tan trousers inappropriate
lunch in my hands, ears etc.

ii.

I sat next to the pig. A patron brought it in mistaking it for a meal and it stayed close to his tarpaulin. He placed it on the table every time he ordered his Sunday lunch 'eating as his subject'. I could smell it like a milkshake tucked into a felt dicepouch. It was absolutely rude! I had no idea what time the last train left. I could sit for hours. The pig's breathing was rolling everywhere hours away and I salted my chips. They were 'piping' hot. He had a small tuft of tobacco coming out of his ear and his haircut, salt and pepper whiskers placed into cigarette paper hanging from his cracked lips, wobbled as the pig nudged him. I sat next to the pig. It was afternoon. I couldn't sleep. Billy was tuning his guitar to a few pigeons he'd been feeding in Piedimonte's. I can't read English in as much as I can blow hot chips and put them into my face my tongue knowing how to guide them along with punctuation. There is in my mouth a ladder (Jorie Graham). Pigs are messy as rugs or, at least, lean in metaphor/self conscious exclamation or bleached hair. I take my straw from its strawberry hide and in no time it's gone as a mouse or heart murmur.

Coda

So I wait here reading Koch drinking in the morning
checking the spelling. I walk to the coast and there are
geese illiterate and barge-like squashed against a bulldozer
wedding. Sand to the summer holiday. I'm nearly, or I
often/never wear swimmers quickly and slip into a wave
$39.95 all over again. Fair trade local milk octopus-flavoured
crisps. Sandals, a can opener – the coast needs an estuary
crank it! bread, zip-lock bags of spinach news or and/or
news words all over the place exerted into the wind
windbreak trees holding the sand, poorly, to the holidays.
I accept ageing. Or running my tongue along the bed of the
ocean I chip a tooth on coral or tooth-like coral and you
crack your knuckles. 'Mahjong and memory' is the lecture,
and gets confusing at the middle distance like/or/if lifting a
spider in the shape of a K out of your hair and putting it into
my birth surname/sincere hope.

Our Russell

Ark-lit Finnish or Danish teak Noah sourced, carefully, spending hours on the Internet late into the night in untrue postures baiting carpel tunnel. The animals shalt not, or shat all over the gleaming polished floorboards immediately. Noah anticipated this and held to the promise of its quality. But only for a few weeks. In a month he became depressed and lost his vision. The 'flood' was a metaphor, he thought, and he began drinking heavily. Certain animals grew wild in captivity and for example the pigs ate Noah's children. He was unable to think his way out of it – the written. And sunlight reflected off a timepiece – the precipice of an expedition on the side of a snowcapped distant mountain in Ararat – and caught Noah's eye. His handkerchief was the chaff bag at the miracle of his children's resurrection which couldn't stop him from heaven. He had conflicts. 'What about a bible?', he said aloud. God is vain but self-aware, he thought.

And Noah was born again high diving. His acrobatics between the cliff and the water were like reef knots.

New York Quay

In an afternoon I watch the waitress push over the mirror runs down the North wall of the restaurant, it goldfishes and the rain patterns our water glasses, nothing is ready. The shops through the window metallic grey as the rain followed by old larger articulated thinking tackle and basketball teeth like 12 wine glasses stranded in the morning, without accents, NY.

Prune Café, Walrus

stood over the half ventilated tattoo
and bit the end of her handkerchief

We understand a great deal about uncomfortable lighting
audible breathing, eradicate croissant

A boxer eating his gloves he was so poor

the cutlery was blunt, as were his sequiturs !

Snail Clogged in the Clay

I played tennis early and then I played late one afternoon in July. I began playing tennis on my own and it was early. When Tim arrived we opened a can of whole tomatoes and like hikers began wading through to the net. A rosella caught in it and we talked about it. We had to raise our voice/tone dove to the bird. Tim watered the court. It was ochre like my corduroy hat. I didn't realise it was warm but a stalactite formed a certain telephone counselling on the already dreamed conversation or daydream.

Tamarisk/Astor

If not for the ocean then for circumstance or time

And if not for time, and time's circulation
then up-drafts that keep a hawk
nourished or dissipated irritation

necessary in a lengthy
acquaintance or drive

If – for this serious beginning, shade unbroken,
walking out past the markers along the cliff edge,
the 'nature' walk, then – we concede
something has happened to beauty…

Jules Olitski spraying canvases
Olives far too salty in the dream of adolescence
School with a love-bite on the neck
– blood summoned and confused as tricked pets

If not for every accident
then the assumptions, coincidence, fortunes

coins grow weak in old wallets or in the
depths of a car seat as things quieten beyond
articulation

A Tusk's Chalking Innocence Against Evening

Rossellini/Lynch, 1986

I get up. I'm wearing your iris
blue lips, have eaten zebra intent

ly, deign to think I could
accomplish, the word fizzing,

again, the square task of art.

How Will I Know When I'm Home?

i.

I had been draped in the maple syrup of early am, and the path to the morning train, and had given myself fifteen minutes to dress and leave. My sleep was inside-out before I put it on, an arms-length reach down each leg simply taught time's lesson. A double knot in my dream. I had a double. Absolutely on the train I could see the morning's poem in a series of scissor images and was sure it would use the scenes as remembered on the free early spacious train but, here, mid-morning, they don't play that way at all. There are no seams. It has adhered to a memory, a shaken beach towel. I spilled sugar all over the kitchen floor on arriving and with no sweeper used the outside of the morning's hybrid awakening to sweeten its way up towards the kitchen sink to make coffee. I had thought to remove the destroyed snail near the front gate as I know Zoë hates that cracked-egg collapse. These were the written lines that had to be shaken into the already existing morning. I was on the train. Two clear seats opposite like coffee cups. Perhaps I'm writing about sleep because of Guest's list poem which was read aloud at some east coast university or such, who was advised by the tenses, quietly spoken pepper breath, of the convenor, about her lines of floss and tendon, arc and cornerstone hazard antler avuncular, lunar, heartened, sleeping, poem, that her end lines might like to confer the whole poem, and under indices anticipate the last piece. But I don't think so. My sleep was so completely honed, laboured-over, and I have no memory of the train pulling away before buying milk and calculating the pause around a road crossing.

ii.

There was no leaving the house. The house was there. It wasn't immobile, wholly, but an address beyond pencils and creamy duck-feathered coloured paper. The letter box clasp always swung open in the wind and we lived there and found our mail sometimes on the lawn, or snail-bitten. I couldn't leave, this day, but dug my way out of the carpet enough to pack a lunch in a silver tiffin and think of the largess of the egg or the eye of the hen on the shiny blunt end of a 2B pencil. When it was typed up I decided to go checking the train times. I was, of course, unlucky and had to kill a good twenty ducks using an old table cloth. It was a turquoise business but the time looks you directly and I was eventually at the five-to-twelve, walking alongside me, and I hopped in. I had left the whole house there frowning by the street in grey daysky inclination. I read the essay at the beginning of the *New American Poetry* to try to orient myself to the second half of my thirties. I won't call it late but I willed the train to skip stations and I did it for enjoyment and the editor also said this. But I didn't believe a word. I just felt the great book in my right hand like my house unread all afternoon if not for robbery or repairs. Our shed, which was only a paragraph or so, long ago, was tidied into a whole dissertation. He even had to remove a piece of grass, ingeniously. I didn't know where to learn. Feathers everywhere. Embarrassing! We shared a coffee when it was over and he had two sons and seemed to know everything with a sly curl of the shifting spanner. We went back years. I was twenty eight. I had breathed between two shoulder blades and fallen into scrub, destroying my chin off a bicycle. We waited for ages at Flinders Station. I hid the cover of the book hard against my left pocket. We turned the page and I went out of the train and up escalators which were tracksuit-top zippers and seemed fine across the tramway pedestrian bikeway, arriving.

iii.

I came through the station dreamily, on with the audio's* tapestry of gargles and intonations, and was without memory as I walked, perfectly attached to the narration and the pace of each commuter. I have nothing to write of what must have been the walk from the station to here, but I rolled out of bed to dress near the heater, and ate dreamily, too, as in half-asleep. We have no telephone. The train came up silently beside me like the memory of an old quarrel. At one point, on the train, the light washed over passages opposite, passengers, and I stared closely at the mauve eyelids of a dozing woman.

***Swann's Way* read by Neville Jason

iv.

I'd been up late staring into Google Earth as it reeled location in for me. And the alarm went off in the room I had slept most of the night in. I was settling Ari when I fell asleep. The morning was extremely heavy. The pillow was deep and the morning was heavy and deep and the alarm irritated me, and I curled over and around Z's warm legs and ignored it and stayed there because of the one cough when I woke, and the three dreams and the vanilla dark of muted early morning. On the train it moved and it moved further and further away from my memory, the morning, mid-morning. I couldn't read a book for long. The congealed ends of lines were crumbs in the bed from yesterday's afternoon toast. I closed my eyes. I opened them and a woman across from me was staring at me. I was concerned for myself, for sleeping, but closed them again, and fell back into the narration of *As I Lay Dying*. The description of the most silent ill person and the hair on her arm, and a horse dropping from a hill, stiff-legged, and the circular, odd beginning of Darl's first go at narration. I spent most of the early morning having breakfast and Ari told of Jupiter crashing in on 'the people'. People in the park, I thought, to write about, freely and in convex prose. We found it, too, weirdly on the tail of a Dali tiger, a week-old pomegranate spilling firework!

v.

We rose together, Ari and I, after dawn and approximately three or four trains, and I delivered him into his mother's side. It was a crumpled sleep, going to him in the night to settle him and then falling asleep. Falling asleep in the night and falling asleep in the night and the quick clock-hand movements needed to shower and scoop muesli and kiss them and leave to tickle the train along or for a long while falling asleep. The swerves and zags loose in the darkened lounge before curtains were invented. The sole lonely muesli and bruising my teeth while falling asleep in the train inventing my way onto the night. I have no memory of getting to the city. Brushed clean early streets.

vi.

Already from the bed and unlocking the necessary doors to the train, before I even got up, or before I woke up. How we wake up but fall down. Imagine the clouds bulbous, always, even on grey days, and mix some oats with sunflower seeds, ancient grains. It actually takes about three minutes to dress, and this I never anticipate. We answer the morning's questions so as the answers get us on the train. And you have to run alongside it as it slows and its dolphin opens and sit near an uxorious conversation. The couples leave each other at Collingwood station and their kiss is pretty long for a goodbye peck and loud! Sneakers out of mud with a large anthology on my lap I feel. Glee! It's pretty silly in size and although it's overcast I can sense a bustling urgency to the city as we skip to complete neglected tasks of elephant, hugely elongated and dangerous pairs of the mind, of a mind, to report them. You three, disembark! I get to the desk and spend good hours fossicking in the muesli to eat it – generic removalist boxes with orange notes and great cardboard efficiencies to taste.

vii.

I had some minutes to doze in the early morning was the width of a bed, the time. Coincidently, and with mattress thickness, the time and space of time of this dozing. I dozed. It came away and floated over and hovered for a good mattress. Not firm, not soft, and there was no snoring. I woke away, alert, and could hear the preparation of Z's hastening exit. It was orange. Not the colour of oranges but the orange of paler fruit such as tangerines, her face, when the artist stayed and painted it with a range of reddy-yellow colours she'd misplaced. It was an 'in-Matisse' moment, I thought, in painting a green fence in Kandinsky-weather the drifts of grass pencilling across the newly-clipped garden lawn. It was a delicacy, those days, having the just-damp lawn clippings flick up over the shins like freckles.

viii.

This morning they were curled insects ancient on a leaf, in sleep. I crossed through rooms and was running for the train, with time in hand, at one point, to gaze deeply at the light of the back lawn. It was muted, as is said, and cold wisps of air entered it and I pulled my elbows close to my ribs in warmth as the train descended from its speed. I sat restlessly returning to old American words of the 1940s and 1950s and sometimes hearing in the 1980s always crackly backgrounds and paint-chipped atmospheres where they swallowed and tried to forget their muscling tongues among the words. I remember the morning like a flickering fluorescent light. I don't even recall where I sat. I tried to move gravel out of my way with my whiskers and the train descended from speed and the nervous wind and the airforce-jet metal of the whole morning in and against my face. I was meaning to arrive with milk and carrot juice, and the glass doors of the entrance were to open on dreaming, but I'd not remembered. It was an un-ticketed film at the end of its short run. I made the train easily. The doors enveloped one part of the morning.

ix.

This morning the alarm was signalled by throwing a net over the sounds pressing through the window, and this thought met the surface of time and the harp of the alarm plucked. Getting out of bed was more like twisting to a prayer posture. The clock was almost completely unfixed out of the shower, which was inexplicably four minutes from sleep. And then the time drained away quickly towards seven and a rush to the train. I had coffee in a small cup, and the time asleep was a dream hidden. Granules of dusty fatigue I tried to wash down the makeshift kitchen sink. Up on an angle and tilted rudely, the kitchen grew out of an early need to mend my appetite with a piece of fruit leather and a pear knife. The veins slid out from under my elbows and we tied them to the fence post. Locals moved in to feed them as birds skipped like splashed paint and the sun insisted on following me into the house again to find my wallet. It was a little blue-frog interval – liver or gullet. I found it in a magazine rack as the memory of it folded away there and passed me like a blimp, unyieldingly slowly, but we, silly still, try to race time. I almost choked on the aftershave. Its peppery musk moving invisibly in the air like an umbrella, entering my lungs the way a horse is saddled.

x.

We made wheat pancakes with our arms out. The cheeks we made sizzled in the breakfast. I woke up ate four pancakes. I drove backwards and forwards, forgetting things and arriving too early to check the furniture. The outer shape of the roundest pancake matched the smile and face we presented to commuters by the time we got back into the car the wind had died down entirely (but only inside the car). Otherwise it was brisk and dogs sailed across the windscreen, ripping the arms of the pancakes out of our mouths. We had to cook keenly and, without hesitation, got out of the car. I had to park four times, but the train station was observed by men in police circumstances blue and a very deep blue and then a blue just three washes deeper than the last. We checked the sky for intelligence. I stepped onto the train and when I arrived in the city the city was on and flows of pedestrians out-smarted the following paperback bookshops slumped and utterly predictable. I found my desk.

Notes

The quote from John Dos Passos comes from his essay, 'The Writer as Technician' (1935). 'Type Slowly' is a Pavement song from their 1997 album *Brighten the Corners* (Matador Records/Capitol Records). 'Black and Brown Blues' is a Silver Jews song from *The Natural Bridge* (Drag City, 1996). *Days in the Wake* is an album by Palace Music (Drag City, 1994). 'The Australian Double' is a line from John Ashbery's collection *Quick Question* (Ecco Press, 2012). The line 'there is in my mouth a ladder' is from a Jorie Graham poem called 'Underneath (13)' from her collection *Swarm* (Ecco Press, 1999). 'Take Your Big Leg Off Me' is from a list of songs in Michael Ondaatje's Buddy Bolden-inspired novel *Coming Through Slaughter* (Marion Boyars,1979). The epigraph to 'Carriages' comes from Michael Ondaatje's poem 'Rock Bottom' in *The Cinnamon Peeler* (Picador, 1989). *Something Has Happened to Beauty* is a text-based public art piece by Brisbane artist Sebastian Moody. Regarding the line, 'Who said that?', in 'Watching Sundance', I remember: in DBC Pierre's *Ludmilla's Broken English* (Faber & Faber, 2006), eyebrows pop 'like crusts of toast'. 'How Will I Know When I'm Home?' is a Laura Jean song from her 2014 self-titled album *Laura Jean* (Chapter Music). This book was originally titled *American Typewriter.*

This project has been assisted by the Commonwealth Government through the Australia Council, its art funding and advisory body.